AF575362

# SOCCER AROUND THE GLOBE

KURT WALDENDORF

childsworld.com

**Published by The Child's World®**
800-599-READ · childsworld.com



**Photography Credits**
Photography Credits
Cover: ©Image Source/Getty Images; ©AlexeyVS/Getty Images: page 3: ©irin-k/Shutterstock; page 5: ©Pictures from History/Getty Images; page 6: ©Kyodo/Newscom; page 7: ©China News Service/Getty Images; page 9: ©Daily Herald Archive/Getty Images; page 10: ©Hulton Archive/Shutterstock; page 11: ©Laurence Griffiths/Getty Images; page 12: ©canbedone/Shutterstock; page 15: ©Focus on Sport/Getty Images; page 16: ©David Madison/Getty Images; page 17: ©Rich Storry/Getty Images; page 19: ©Stu Foster/Getty; page 20: Eurasia Sport Images/Getty Images; page 21: ©Christian Kaspar-Bartke/Getty Images; page 23: ©SLSK Photography/Shutterstock; page 25: ©Romain Baird/Shutterstock: page 26: ©Hector Vivas—FIFA/Getty Images; page 27: ©Hector Vivas—FIFA/Getty Images; page 28: ©lazyllama/Shutterstock; page 29: ©Anne-Christine Poujoulat/Getty Images

**ISBN Information**
ISBN 9781503894242 (Reinforced Library Binding)
ISBN 9781503895225 (Portable Document Format)
ISBN 9781503896048 (Online Multi-user eBook)
ISBN 9781503896864 (Electronic Publication)

**LCCN**
2024941369

Printed in the United States of America

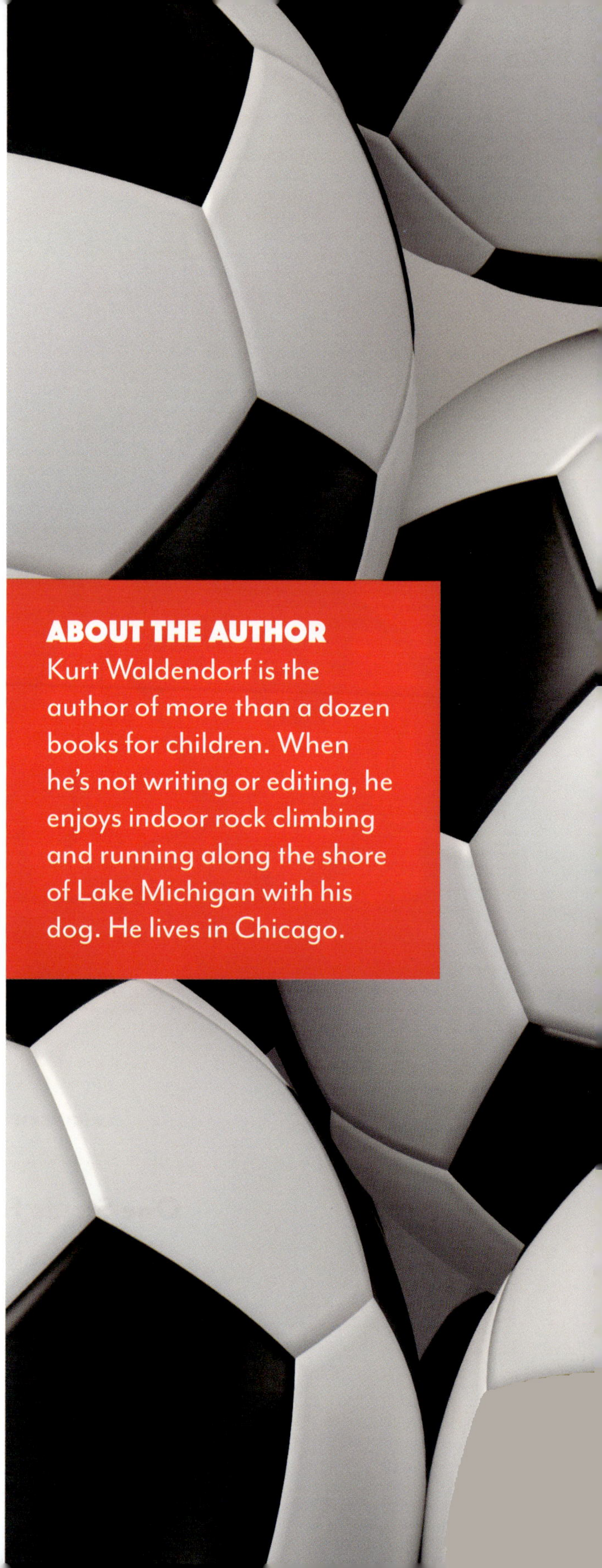

## ABOUT THE AUTHOR

Kurt Waldendorf is the author of more than a dozen books for children. When he's not writing or editing, he enjoys indoor rock climbing and running along the shore of Lake Michigan with his dog. He lives in Chicago.

# CONTENTS

CHAPTER ONE

# ANCIENT GAMES

Soccer is the most popular sport in the world today. More athletes play the game and more fans watch its matches than any other sport. Soccer is known as football in much of the world. Because soccer is so popular, it is also called the global game.

Soccer as we know it today has a long history. The rules were created less than 200 years ago. But the sport is part of an even longer history. The tradition of soccer-like games goes back more than 2,000 years. The earliest known example was *cuju*, or "kick-ball." It was first played in China during the Han **dynasty** (206 BC–220 AD). Like soccer, cuju involved two teams. Players used their legs, feet, and hips to pass a ball. Unlike soccer, the players could not let the ball touch the ground. Teams took turns trying to kick the ball through a hoop hanging high above the middle of the field.

Although there were many versions of cuju, they all had one thing in common—players could not touch the ball with their hands.

## COOPERATIVE KEMARI

**In Japan, people played a soccer-like game called kemari as early as around 644 AD. Kemari was a cooperative game. Players passed a ball around a small field without using their hands. The aim was to complete as many passes as possible while keeping the ball off the ground. There was a tree in each corner of the court. This made the passes harder to complete.**

Cuju started as a way for soldiers to stay fit. Over time, it became a **pastime** for everyday people. Men, women, and children all played. During the Song dynasty (960–1279 AD), **professional** leagues formed. Then, during the Ming dynasty (1368–1644 AD), the sport began to be played less. People turned to other games. Soldiers found new ways to train.

Cuju was one of many ancient ball games. In Japan, people played a similar game called kemari. Early civilizations in Greece and the Americas had their own ball games. These games help explain why soccer is so popular today. Like these ancient sports, soccer gives athletes a way to stay fit and work as a team. For fans, it brings the excitement of watching players achieve amazing things using little more than a ball, a goal, and their feet.

Today, cuju is mostly played to entertain tourists who visit historic sites in China.

CHAPTER TWO

# SOCCER IN EUROPE

Soccer-like games first appeared in Europe in the 1100s. People in England played "folk football." Sometimes whole towns played. Each team tried to toss or kick a ball into the other team's goal. Folk football rules were different from place to place. Some towns allowed players to carry the ball with their hands. Others did not. Some games were very physical. Others had rules against pushing and tackling.

In 1863, the first soccer **association** formed in the United Kingdom. It divided folk football games into two sports. The more physical game became **rugby**. The game that focused on speed and quickness became soccer. In 1872, the association set a standard weight and size for the soccer ball. The group banned soccer players from carrying the ball. Modern soccer was born.

Residents of Ashbourne, a city in England, have been playing a street soccer tournament known as the Royal Shrovetide Football Match every spring since 1667.

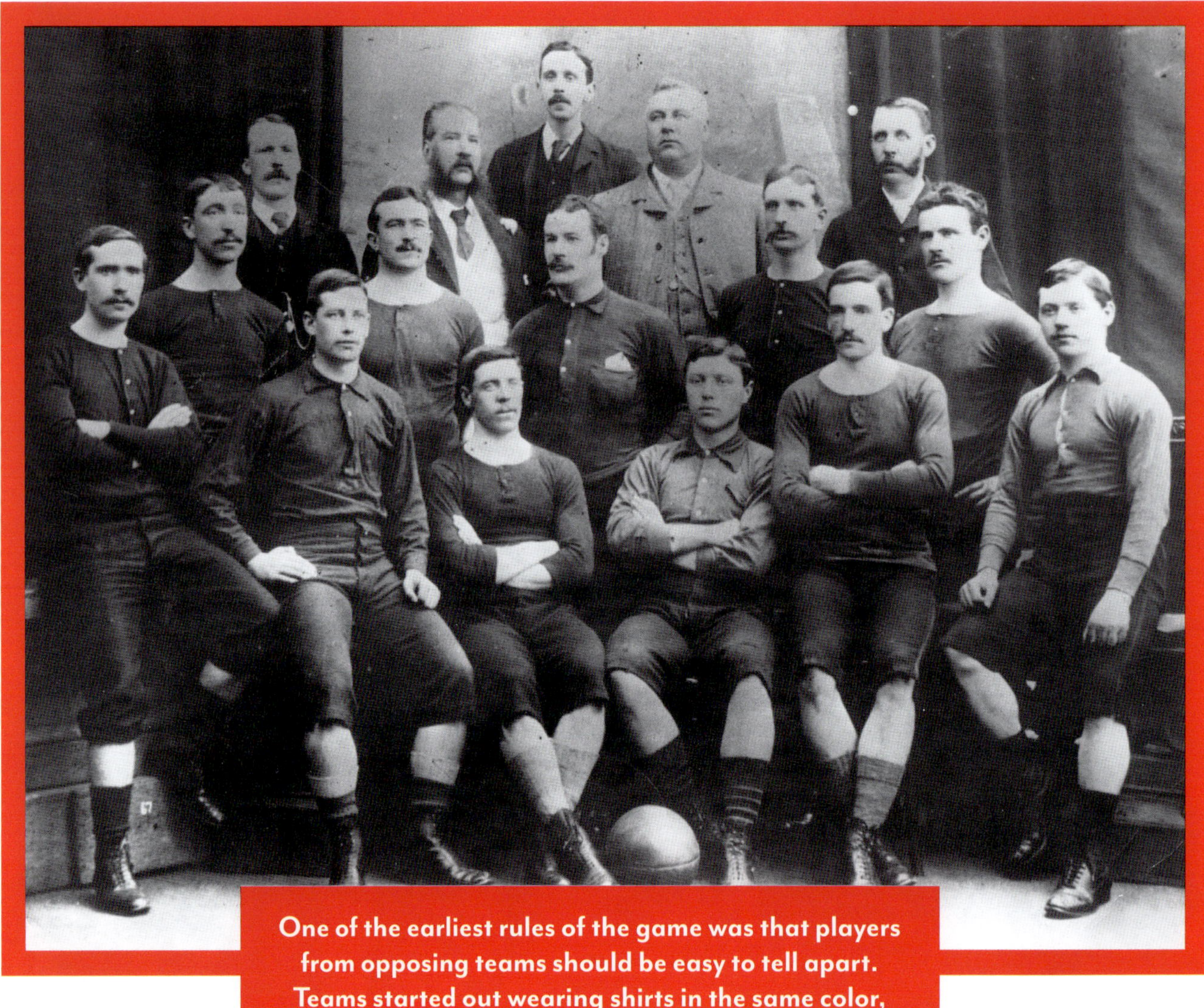

**One of the earliest rules of the game was that players from opposing teams should be easy to tell apart. Teams started out wearing shirts in the same color, which later led to matching jerseys and shorts.**

Soccer spread quickly through the United Kingdom in the late 1800s. At the time, many people were moving to cities to work in factories. Workers were looking for new pastimes. They formed factory teams. Church and school teams formed, too.

Transportation was getting better. People could more easily travel to see matches. Fans began to pay to see their favorite teams. In 1888, the first professional soccer league started in the United Kingdom.

The game also spread quickly across Europe. English school teachers brought soccer to Germany in 1874. The game arrived in France in the early 1900s. The Netherlands formed its first soccer league in 1889.

In 1904, an international soccer organization was formed. It was called the Fédération Internationale de Football Association (FIFA). Soccer is called football in many parts of the world. FIFA oversees international soccer to this day. The group sets the game's rules and organizes tournaments.

Today, Europe is home to some of the best soccer leagues in the world. Players from around the globe train hard to get a chance to compete on European **club teams**. The top leagues are known as the Big Five. They include the Premier League in England, La Liga in Spain, Bundesliga in Germany, Ligue 1 in France, and Serie A in Italy.

The top clubs from across Europe play in a club championship. These events are organized by the Union of European Football Associations (UEFA). The first big championship was the European Cup. It began in 1955. Today, the tournament is called the UEFA Champions League. Each year, the top 36 clubs compete. The winner is named European club champion.

# EUROPEAN CLUB CHAMPIONS

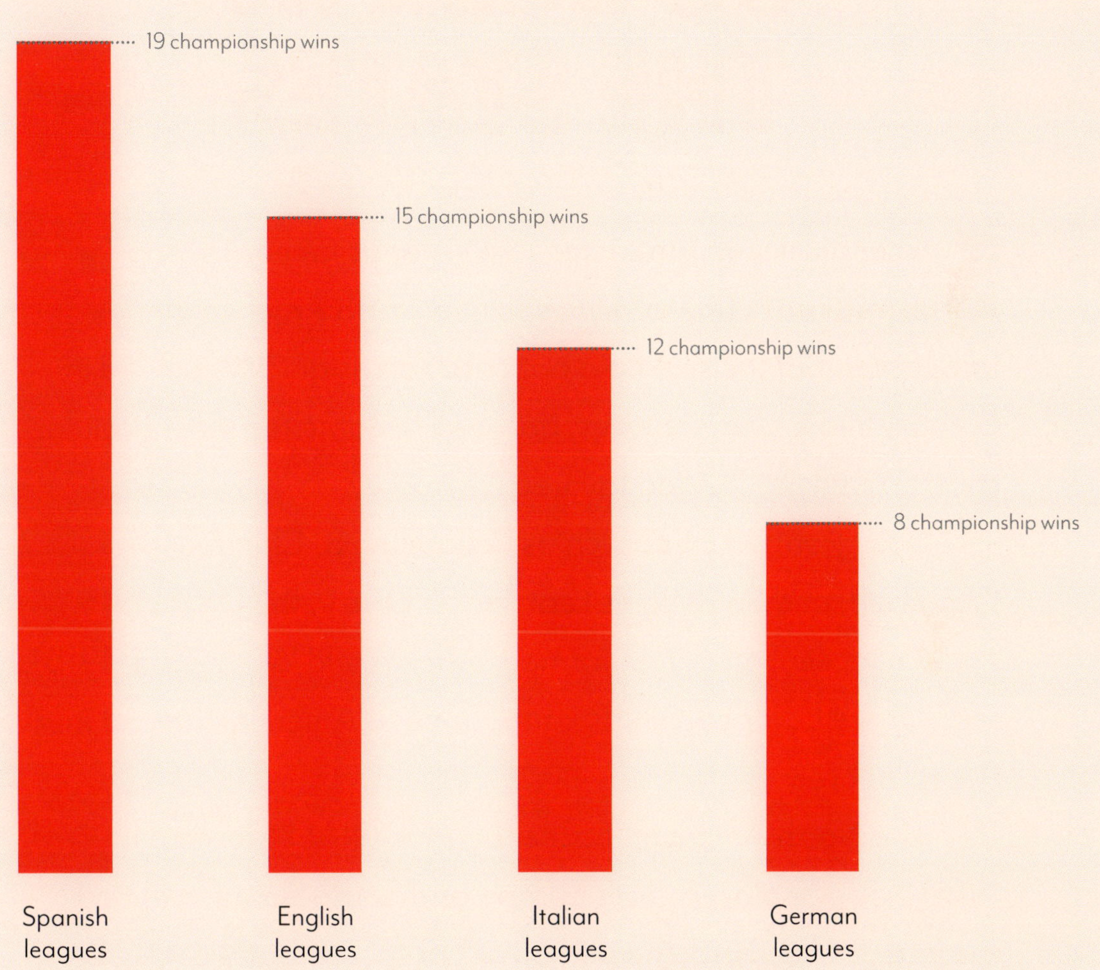


**Clubs from Spanish leagues have won the competition 19 times. Clubs from English leagues have won it 15 times, followed by Italy at 12 and Germany at eight.**

CHAPTER THREE

# SOCCER IN THE STATES

Soccer quickly spread across the Atlantic Ocean. European **immigrants** brought the sport to North America in the late 1850s. But the sport did not catch on as quickly as it did in Europe. In the United States, baseball became the most popular sport. People in Canada favored ice hockey.

Immigrants in cities such as Philadelphia, Chicago, Cleveland, and Saint Louis kept soccer alive in the US. In 1913, the US Soccer Federation formed. After World War I (1914–1918), many more European immigrants came to America. Interest in the sport grew.

The North American Soccer League (NASL) formed in 1968. Popular players from Europe and South America joined the league. The NASL helped grow US soccer. But a consistent fanbase did not develop. The league shut down in 1984.

**Brazilian star Pelé played three seasons with the New York Cosmos from 1975 until 1977. Many Americans became more interested in soccer as a result of his time with the team.**

The 1999 Women's World Cup final set an attendance record at the time for the largest crowd at a women's sporting event. More than 90,000 people were at the game.

US soccer got a boost in the early 1990s. The country hosted the 1994 World Cup. Americans watched the world's top **national teams** compete. Across nine cities, more people attended the matches than any World Cup before. In 1996, a new US league started, Major League Soccer (MLS). Unlike the NASL, MLS focused on local talent. It built up strong fan bases in US cities.

American soccer got another boost in 1999. The US Women's National Team won the Women's World Cup. Players from around the world came to play in US women's leagues. The National Women's Soccer League (NWSL) began in 2013. It is one of the best women's leagues in the world. Today, MLS and the NWSL continue to grow. As of 2024, there are 29 MLS clubs. The NWSL has 14.

## ATTRACTING GLOBAL STARS

**Many international stars have played in US leagues. In 1975 Brazilian star Pelé joined the New York Cosmos of the NASL. In 2023, Lionel Messi from Argentina joined Inter Miami of MLS. Both players are among the best of all time. Pelé and Messi each led their clubs to major wins. They also helped bring attention to US soccer.**

CHAPTER FOUR

# FÚTBOL IN CENTRAL AND SOUTH AMERICA

Soccer came to Central America in the late 1880s. Unlike its neighbors to the north, Mexico adopted the sport quickly. Its first league formed in 1903. A league followed in Costa Rica in 1921. Soccer spread more slowly in the rest of the region. In Nicaragua, El Salvador, and Honduras, baseball was more popular. In the Caribbean, people preferred **cricket**.

The **Confederation** of North, Central America, and Caribbean Association Football (CONCACAF) formed in 1961. It organizes the region's club championship, the Champions Cup. Clubs from Mexico's top league, Liga MX, have dominated. Liga MX clubs have won 38 championships. Clubs from Costa Rica have won six titles. US clubs have won the tournament three times. In 2025, CONCACAF will host its first women's club championship. The tournament will include 11 clubs from seven countries.

Mexican goalkeeper Jorge Campos was well-known for his ability to play multiple positions—he even scored more than 30 goals in his career!

**Marta has been named FIFA World Player of the Year six times and is Brazil's top goal-scorer of all time.**

In South America, immigrants first brought the sport to Argentina. A league formed in 1893. Leagues followed in Brazil, Colombia, and Uruguay. By the 1930s, soccer was part of popular culture in many South American countries. It became a common pastime in large cities.

Soon, local players were playing at top levels. Many competed in Europe's best leagues. South America also developed its own top leagues. Today, Serie A in Brazil and Primera División in Argentina are among the best in the world.

The Confederación Sudamericana de Fútbol (CONMEBOL) oversees competition across South America. Its club championship is called Copa Libertadores. Clubs from Argentina have won the championship 25 times. Clubs from Brazil have won 23 titles.

In 2009, a South American women's club championship began. The tournament includes the top 16 women's clubs from across South America. Brazil has dominated. Its clubs have won 12 of the 15 titles.

## GROWING IN THE GAME

**Soccer is the most popular sport in South America. But the women's game has not been as successful. CONMEBOL is trying to change that. In 2017, it began organizing youth tournaments for girls. In 2019, it created a new rule. If a club wanted to take part in the men's club championship, it must also have a women's club.**

CHAPTER FIVE

# ON THE WORLD STAGE

As soccer spread around the world, FIFA set up a global tournament. Every four years, the top national teams compete in the World Cup. During the tournament, clubs pause their schedules. They allow players to compete for their home nations.

The first World Cup took place in 1930. The country where soccer began, the United Kingdom, did not participate. It had left FIFA in 1928. The country's soccer association did not like FIFA's growing role. But in 1946, the United Kingdom rejoined FIFA. Today, there are 211 FIFA associations. These are grouped into six confederations. There is UEFA in Europe, CONCACAF in North and Central America, and CONMEBOL in South America. There is also the Confederation of African Football (CAF) and the Asian Football Confederation (AFC). The Oceania Football Confederation (OFC) represents Australia and countries in the South Pacific. Each confederation holds its own tournaments. The top national teams represent each confederation in the World Cup.

The World Cup is played in a different place every four years. The 2023 Women's World Cup took place in Australia and New Zealand, and the 2022 Men's World Cup was held in Qatar.

Today, the Men's World Cup is the most popular sporting event in the world. Billions of viewers tune in to watch. Early on, the Men's World Cup was played in Europe or South America. Over the years, it has been played on every continent except Australia and Antarctica. The most successful men's team has been Brazil, which has won five World Cups. Germany and Italy each have four titles. Argentina has three.

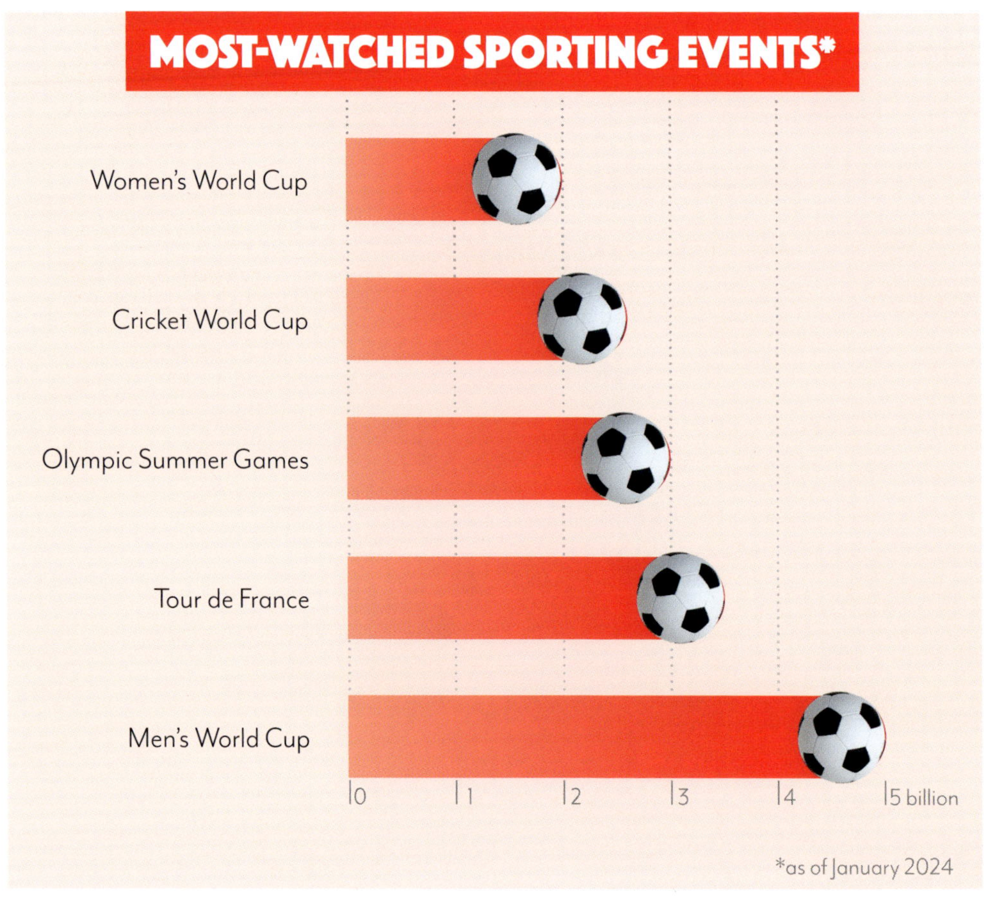

The Women's World Cup began in 1991. It is held one year after the Men's World Cup. The US Women's National Team has won the title four times. Germany has won it twice. Norway, Japan, and Spain each have one Women's World Cup title.

**Alex Morgan has led the United States to two World Cup wins and was one of the first female players to appear on the cover of a video game—FIFA 16.**

CHAPTER SIX

# SOCCER AT THE OLYMPICS

The second-biggest soccer event takes place at the Olympic Games. Like the sport of soccer, the Olympics have a long history. The first Olympics were held in ancient Greece in 776 BC. It included just one competition, a footrace. Over time, the Olympics grew to include many different competitions. The original Olympic Games lasted until about 394 AD.

The modern Olympics have been played since 1896. A man named Pierre de Coubertin led the effort to bring the games back. He saw the Olympics as a way to unite people. The games are a celebration of what humans have in common. Men's soccer first appeared at the Olympics in 1900. The competition takes place every four years with the World Cup taking place in between.

The Olympics give athletes an opportunity to show off their skills while promoting kindness and friendship between countries around the world.

## THE OLYMPIC FLAG

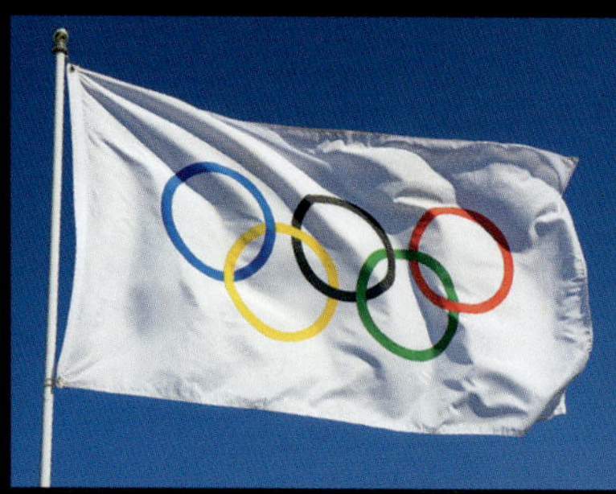

**The Olympic flag represents Olympic values. The connected rings indicate the continents coming together. The colors black, blue, yellow, white, red, and green represent the many flags of the countries that take part. Today, athletes from more than 200 countries compete in the summer Olympic Games.**

For many years, the Olympic Games were for **amateur** athletes. This was to keep the focus on **sportsmanship** rather than on money. But after professional sports became more popular, the rule changed. In 1986, Olympic organizers said they would allow pro athletes to participate. Still, there are differences between soccer at the Olympics and at the World Cup. In Olympic soccer, there is an age rule. Men's teams can have only three players above 23 years old. Also, the tournament is not a FIFA event. Clubs are not required to let players participate. Many men's national teams compete without their biggest stars. This allows younger players to shine. Women's soccer was added to the Olympics in 1996. There are no age rules for the women's game.

**Brazil won the gold medal for men's soccer at both the 2016 and 2020 Olympics.**

Today, the sport of soccer continues to grow. China, India, and the United States are the countries with the biggest populations in the world. In these places, more people are playing and watching soccer than ever. The future of the global game is bright.

# GLOSSARY

**amateur** (AM-uh-chur) taking part in a sport for pleasure, not for pay

**association** (uh-soh-see-AY-shuhn) a governing body that unites smaller bodies, such as leagues

**club teams** (KLUB TEEMZ) teams that represent an organization, often including players from many different cities or countries

**confederation** (kun-fed-uh-RAY-shuhn) a governing body that unites smaller bodies, such as associations

**cricket** (KRIK-eht) a game played on a large field with bats, ball, and wickets by two teams of 11 players

**dynasty** (DY-nuh-stee) a succession of rulers of the same line of descent

**immigrant** (IHM-eh-grahnt) a person who comes to a country to live there

**national teams** (NASH-uh-nul TEEMZ) teams that represent a country, in which all players are from a single nation

**pastime** (PASS-tym) an activity that makes time pass agreeably

**professional** (proh-FESH-uh-nahl) taking part in a sport for money

**rugby** (RUG-bee) a game between two teams in which play is continuous and the team that has the ball may run with it, kick it, or pass it sideways or backward but is not allowed to block or make forward passes

**sportsmanship** (SPORTS-man-ship) fair play, respect for opponents, and gracious behavior in winning or losing

## FAST FACTS

- More than 250 million people play soccer across more than 200 countries.
- The World Cup Final match draws around 1.5 billion viewers. The Super Bowl brings in about 120 million viewers.
- Hungary and Great Britain lead Olympic men's soccer with three gold medals. The US women lead with four golds.
- Brazil's Marta has the most Women's World Cup goals with 17. Germany's Miroslav Klose holds the men's record with 16.
- In matches against Mexico, the US Men's National Team is 38 and 25 with 17 draws. The US women are 41 and 2 with one draw.

## ONE STRIDE FURTHER

- Based on what you've learned from this book, why do you think soccer became the most popular game in the world? Think about your answers and have a friend do the same. Compare your lists.
- Ask friends and family members about their favorite sports. Keep track and make a graph to see which sport wins out.
- Players train hard to make it to the top leagues in the world. Write a paragraph describing the skills and attitudes you think it takes to reach the highest level.

# FIND OUT MORE

## IN THE LIBRARY


Davidson, B. Keith. *MLS*. New York, NY: Crabtree, 2022.

*Everything You Need to Know about Soccer*. New York, NY: DK Children, 2024.

Lowe, Alexander. *G.O.A.T. Soccer Midfielders.* Minneapolis, MN: Lerner, 2022.

Lowe, Alexander. *G.O.A.T. Soccer Strikers*. Minneapolis, MN: Lerner, 2022.


## ON THE WEB

Visit our website for links about soccer around the globe:
**childsworld.com/links**

*Note to Parents, Caregivers, Teachers, and Librarians: We routinely verify our web links to make sure they are safe and active sites. So encourage your readers to check them out!*

# INDEX